Unit Information – Unit IC 01 is aimed at health and social care professionals working in a variety of settings. The unit comprises the following learning outcomes:

- LO1 Understand roles and responsibilities in the prevention and control of infections (page 3)
- LO2 Understand legislation and policies relating to prevention and control of infections (page 5)
- LO3 Understand systems and procedures relating to the prevention and control of infections (page 7)
- LO4 Understand the importance of risk assessment in relation to the prevention and control of infections (page 10)
- LO5 Understand the importance of using personal protective equipment (PPE) in the prevention and control of infections (page 14)

- LO6 Understand the importance of good personal hygiene in the prevention [...])

Key Wor[...] [...]ow are inclu[...] criteria a[...] **knowled[...]**

Define – [...]
Describe – to give an account that includes details
Explain – to give an account that includes providing reasons, with examples of how, when, what and/or why
Outline – to provide brief details
State – to provide clear and brief details
Understand – to know the meaning

The key word identified below is included within this unit's assessment criteria and relates to demonstrating **skills**. Its meaning is as follows:

Demonstrate – to show

LO1 Understand roles and responsibilities in the prevention and control of infections

To demonstrate that **Learning Outcome 1** has been achieved you must be able to evidence **your knowledge and understanding** of:

- Employees' roles and responsibilities in relation to the prevention and control of infection (AC1.1).
- Employers' roles and responsibilities in relation to the prevention and control of infection (AC1.2).

AC1.1 Explain employees' roles and responsibilities in relation to the prevention and control of infection

All health and social care workers have duties and legal obligations in relation to preventing and controlling infections; most of their legal obligations about infection control are included in the Health and Safety at Work Act 1974. All health and social care workers are required to work in ways that protect individuals, staff and visitors from harm, including from potential infection. There is a range of infection control practices – referred to as standard infection control precautions – that must be applied by employees, for example when in contact with blood or body fluids, to minimise the risk of infections. Standard infection control precautions include good hand washing and personal hygiene, the use of protective clothing and equipment and safe handling of waste and spillages that may occur.

AC1.2 Explain employers' responsibilities in relation to the prevention and control of infection

Under the Health and Safety at Work Act 1974, employers also are responsible for preventing and controlling infections. Their responsibilities include making all employees aware of how infections can be prevented through, for example, providing them with information and having in place up-to-date policies and procedures, training and supervision of their work practices. Employers are also responsible for ensuring that risk assessments are carried out so that it is possible to identify any work tasks that may have the potential to spread infection.

Knowledge Activity ACs1.1, 1.2

Provide an explanation, with examples, of employees' roles and responsibilities and employers' responsibilities in relation to the prevention and control of infection. You may find it useful to reference the Health and Safety Executive's website: www.hse.gov. uk (HSE is the national independent regulator for health and safety in the workplace) or the infection prevention and control procedures in your work setting for more information.

- Employees' roles and responsibilities in relation to the prevention and control of infection:

....

....

....

....

....

....

....

- Employers' responsibilities in relation to the prevention and control of infection:

....

....

....

....

....

....

....

LO2 Understand legislation and policies relating to prevention and control of infections

To demonstrate that **Learning Outcome 2** has been achieved you must be able to evidence **your knowledge and understanding** of:

- Current legislation and regulatory body standards that are relevant to the prevention and control of infection (AC2.1).
- Local and organisational policies relevant to the prevention and control of infection (AC2.2).

AC2.1 Outline current legislation and regulatory body standards that are relevant to the prevention and control of infection

As you learned in ACs 1.1 and 1.2, employees' and employers' responsibilities in relation to infection prevention and control are governed by different pieces of legislation; the main one being the Health and Safety at Work Act 1974. Regulators such as the National Institute for Health and Care Excellence (NICE) and Skills for Health have also developed standards that provide national guidance and advice on good practices to prevent and control infections.

Knowledge Activity AC2.1

Identify three examples of current legislation and three examples of regulatory body standards that are relevant to the prevention and control of infection and then provide an outline for each. You may find it useful to reference the Health and Safety Executive's website: www.hse.gov.uk:

Current prevention and control of infection legislation	Regulatory body standards for the prevention and control of infection
1)	1) ....
2)	2) ....
3)	3) ....

AC2.2 Describe local and organisational policies that are relevant to the prevention and control of infection

As well as legislation and regulatory body standards, a number of health and safety and infection prevention and control policies have been developed by organisations and across regions and services in health and social care. These set out the expectations and roles of employees and employers for the prevention and control of infection.

Knowledge Activity AC2.2

Identify three examples of local policies and three examples of organisational policies that are relevant to the prevention and control of infection. Provide a description for each. You may find it useful to reference the infection prevention and control procedures in your work setting for more information.

Local policies	Organisational policies
1)	1) ....
2)	2) ....
3)	3) ....

LO3 Understand systems and procedures relating to the prevention and control of infections

To demonstrate that **Learning Outcome 3** has been achieved you must be able to evidence **your knowledge and understanding** of:

- Procedures and systems relevant to the prevention and control of infection (AC3.1).

- The potential impact of an outbreak of infection on the individual and the organisation (AC3.2).

AC3.1 Describe procedures and systems relevant to the prevention and control of infection

All work settings are required to have in place procedures and systems that protect everyone who lives, works and visits there from infections. The diagram below identifies what some of these procedures and systems may include.

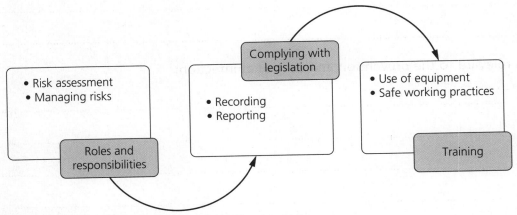

Figure 1 Procedures and systems that protect from infections

Knowledge Activity AC3.1

Identify three examples of procedures and three examples of systems that are relevant to the prevention and control of infection, and then provide a description for each. You may find it useful to reference the infection prevention and control procedures in your work setting for more information.

Procedures relevant to the prevention and control of infection:

1) ....
....
....
....
....
....

2) ....
....
....

3) ....
....
....
....
....
....

Systems relevant to the prevention and control of infection:

1) ....
....
....
....
....
....
....

2) ....
....
....
....
....
....

3) ....
....
....
....
....
....

AC3.2 Explain the potential impact of an outbreak of infection on the individual and the organisation

Not complying with procedures and safe systems of working can lead to an outbreak of infection. This can have a serious impact not only for the infected individual but also on the organisation. Read through the table below, which includes some of the ways that an outbreak of infection can impact on both individuals and organisations.

Impact of an outbreak of infection on the individual	Impact of an outbreak of infection on the organisation
• Illness • Death • Stress • Disruption to day-to-day activities	• Staff shortages • Reduced services • Increased costs • Damage to reputation

Workplace Reflection

Reflect on the health or social care setting where you work and think about:

• the potential impact of an outbreak of infection on the individual
• the potential impact of an outbreak of infection on your work setting.

Knowledge Activity AC3.2

In your own words, explain with examples how an outbreak of infection can affect:

• the individual:

....
....
....
....
....

• the organisation:

....
....
....
....
....

LO4 Understand the importance of risk assessment in relation to the prevention and control of infections

To demonstrate that **Learning Outcome 4** has been achieved you must be able to evidence **your knowledge and understanding** of:

- The term 'risk' (AC4.1).
- The potential risks of infection within the workplace (AC4.2).
- The process of carrying out a risk assessment (AC4.3).
- The importance of carrying out a risk assessment (AC4.4).

AC4.1 Define the term 'risk'

In relation to infection prevention and control the term risk is used to describe the likelihood of the spread of infection occurring, for example through unsafe work practices.

Knowledge Activity AC4.1

In your own words, provide a definition of the term risk in relation to infection prevention and control.

....

....

....

....

....

....

AC4.2 Outline potential risks of infection within the workplace

Infections can be caused and can spread within the workplace. Potential risks of infection can arise in different areas within the work setting (e.g. in bathrooms), in relation to tasks being carried out (e.g. those that involve contact with bodily fluids) and in relation to individuals who may be more susceptible to infection (e.g. those with low immune systems).

Knowledge Activity AC4.2

Provide an outline of three potential risks of infection within your work setting.

1) ....

....

....

....

....

2) ....
....
....
....
....
....

3) ....
....
....
....
....
....

AC4.3 Describe the process of carrying out a risk assessment

Risk assessment plays an important part in preventing and controlling infections and is a continuous process. Employers are responsible for carrying out risk assessments and employees are responsible for complying with the risk assessment process. The risk assessment process consists of the following steps:

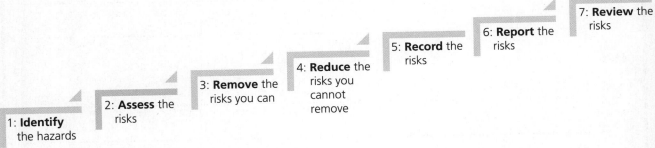

1: **Identify** the hazards

2: **Assess** the risks

3: **Remove** the risks you can

4: **Reduce** the risks you cannot remove

5: **Record** the risks

6: **Report** the risks

7: **Review** the risks

Figure 2 The risk assessment process

Knowledge Activity AC4.3

Using the steps identified in the diagram above, describe the process of carrying out a risk assessment.

Step 1

....
....

....
....
....
....

Step 2

....
....
....
....
....
....

Step 3

....
....
....
....
....
....

Step 4

....
....
....
....
....
....

Step 5

....
....

....

....

....

....

Step 6

....

....

....

....

....

Step 7

....

....

....

....

....

AC4.4 Explain the importance of carrying out a risk assessment

Carrying out risk assessments is important for:

- preventing and controlling infections
- complying with legislation
- complying with local and organisational policies and procedures.

Knowledge Activity AC4.4

Provide an explanation, with examples, of the importance of carrying out a risk assessment in relation to infection prevention and control.

....

....

....

....

....

....

....

....

....

....

LO5 Understand the importance of using personal protective equipment (PPE) in the prevention and control of infections

To demonstrate that **Learning Outcome 5** has been achieved you must be able to evidence **your knowledge and understanding** of:

- The different types of PPE (AC5.2).
- The reasons for use of PPE (AC5.3).
- Current relevant regulations and legislation relating to PPE (AC5.4).
- Employees' responsibilities regarding the use of PPE (AC5.5).
- Employers' responsibilities regarding the use of PPE (AC5.6).
- The correct practice in the application and removal of PPE (AC5.7).
- The correct procedure for disposal of used PPE (AC5.8).

Also **your skills** in:

- The correct use of PPE (AC5.1).

AC5.1 Demonstrate the correct use of PPE

Personal protective equipment (PPE) protects us all against infections when it is used correctly, as it creates barriers between our bodies and those of others. Some examples of PPE used in health or social care settings include uniforms, gloves and aprons.

Using PPE correctly involves choosing the right PPE for the task to be completed, for example using blue-coloured disposable gloves when preparing food and white-coloured disposable gloves when assisting an individual with their personal care. Ensuring the PPE fits correctly is also important: too big and it might fall off; too small and it might rip. Following the correct procedures for using and disposing of PPE is also important, as not doing so can mean that it is no longer effective in the prevention and control of infections.

Workplace Reflection

Reflect on the health or social care setting where you work and think about:

- the PPE you use
- how you use it
- why you use it in this way.

Assessment Activity AC5.1

For the assessment activity your assessor will observe you in your work setting. You will need to show your assessor that you are able to use PPE correctly. To do this you will need to be observed working; you must agree this with your manager.

AC5.2 Describe different types of PPE

There are many different types of personal protective equipment (PPE). The diagram below identifies some of these.

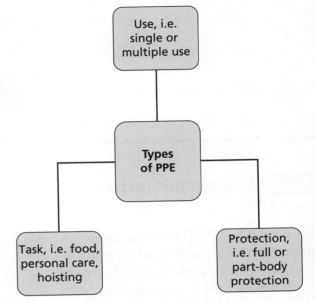

Figure 3 Different types of personal protective equipment

Knowledge Activity AC5.2

Describe three different types of PPE.

Type 1

Type 2

Type 3

....

....

....

....

....

....

AC5.3 Explain the reasons for use of PPE

As you read in AC5.1, personal protective equipment (PPE) protects us all against infections as it creates barriers between our bodies and those of others, such as individuals, colleagues and visitors to our work setting. Using PPE is important for the following reasons:

P Protection from infections

P Prevention of the spread of infections

E Everyone's safety can be maintained

Read through **Case Scenario: Joshua** and consider why he uses PPE in his job role.

Case Scenario: Joshua

Joshua is a support worker who provides one-to-one support to Ronald, who lives at home with his parents. Joshua has eczema and therefore ensures he always wears gloves when supporting Ronald to prepare his lunch. In the evenings, Joshua supports Ronald to have a shower before going to bed and ensures he always wears gloves and an apron to do so.

Workplace Reflection

Reflect on the health or social care setting where you work and think about:

● the individuals to whom you provide care or support

● the reasons for the use of PPE.

Knowledge Activity AC5.3

Explain the reasons for the use of PPE.

....

....

....

....

....

....

....

....

....

....

....

....

....

....

....

....

AC5.4 State current relevant regulations and legislation relating to PPE

Regulations such as the Personal Protective Equipment at Work Regulations 1992 and the Personal Protective Equipment Regulations 2002, as well as legislation such as the Health and Safety at Work Act 1974, govern how PPE is to be used, maintained and disposed of safely. In health or social care settings the legislation in place requires that PPE must be supplied free of charge, and the regulations require that PPE must meet a certain quality standard and that training be provided in its use.

Knowledge Activity AC5.4

State the current relevant regulations relating to PPE.

....

....

....

....

....

....

State the current relevant legislation relating to PPE.

....

....

....

....

....

....

AC5.5 Describe employees' responsibilities regarding the use of PPE

The legislation and regulations outlined in AC5.4 set out the responsibilities regarding the use of PPE for both employees and employers.

Some of the key responsibilities for employees regarding the use of PPE include:

- using PPE provided correctly
- attending training on the use of PPE
- checking PPE before it is used
- reporting difficulties in using PPE
- following their work setting's policies and procedures.

AC5.6 Describe employers' responsibilities regarding the use of PPE

Some of the key responsibilities of employers regarding the use of PPE include:

- assessing the use of PPE
- providing training on its use
- providing information on its use
- providing guidance on its use
- ensuring PPE is available when required
- ensuring PPE is maintained correctly
- ensuring PPE is stored correctly.

Workplace Reflection

Reflect on the health or social care setting where you work and think about:

- your responsibilities regarding the use of PPE
- your employer's responsibilities regarding the use of PPE.

Knowledge Activity ACs5.5, 5.6

Describe the responsibilities of both employees and employers regarding the use of PPE.

- Responsibilities of employees:

....

....

....

....

....

....

....

- Responsibilities of employers:

....

....

....

....

....

....

....

AC5.7 Describe the correct practice in the application and removal of PPE

It is important when applying and removing PPE that you follow your work setting's policies and procedures, as well as the manufacturer's instructions, for doing so.

Read through **Case Scenario: Margarita** and identify how many correct practices she follows when applying and removing PPE.

Case Scenario: Margarita

Margarita is a care worker, and she will be supporting Martha with her breakfast this morning. Before doing so, Margarita washes and dries her hands thoroughly and then puts on a disposable apron by placing the neck strap on first and then tying the waist straps behind her back. Margarita then puts on a pair of disposable gloves, checking first that they are not torn.

After supporting Martha with her breakfast Margarita carefully removes her apron by pulling on the neck strap and waist straps, and then disposes of it in the clinical waste bin. Margarita then proceeds to remove her gloves by pulling on the cuff so as to turn one, then the other, inside out in order to ensure that her hands do not touch the used sides of the gloves. She disposes of them carefully and immediately in the clinical waste bin. Margarita then washes and dries her hands thoroughly.

Knowledge Activity AC5.7

Describe the correct practice in the application of two types of PPE.

1) ....

....

....

....

....

....

2) ....

....

....

....

....

Describe the correct practice in the removal of two types of PPE.

1) ....

....

....

....

....

....

2) ....

....

....

....

....

AC5.8 Describe the correct procedure for the disposal of used PPE

Disposing of used PPE must also be done in line with your work setting's policies and procedures, and in line with the manufacturer's instructions. The procedures to follow will vary depending on what type of PPE is being disposed of; the diagram below includes some of the key points that disposal procedures must include.

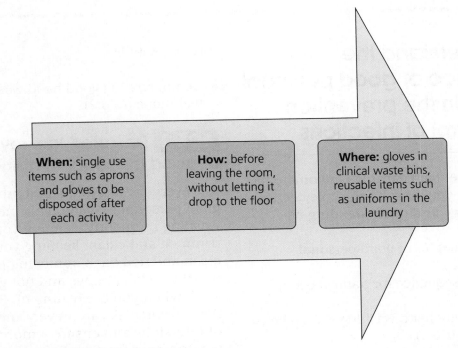

When: single use items such as aprons and gloves to be disposed of after each activity

How: before leaving the room, without letting it drop to the floor

Where: gloves in clinical waste bins, reusable items such as uniforms in the laundry

Figure 4 Key points of disposal procedures

Knowledge Activity AC5.8

Find out about and read through your work setting's policy and procedure for the disposal of used PPE. Describe below in your own words the correct procedure to follow for disposing of used PPE.

....

....

....

....

....

....

....

....

....

....

LO6 Understand the importance of good personal hygiene in the prevention and control of infections

To demonstrate that **Learning Outcome 6** has been achieved you must be able to evidence **your knowledge and understanding** of:

- The key principles of good personal hygiene (AC6.1).
- The correct sequence for hand washing (AC6.3).
- When and why hand washing should be carried out (AC6.4).
- The types of products that should be used for hand washing (AC6.5).
- The correct procedures that relate to skincare (AC6.6).

Also **your skills** in:

- Demonstrating good hand washing technique (AC6.2).

AC6.1 Describe the key principles of good personal hygiene

It is everyone's responsibility to maintain good personal hygiene. This includes washing frequently, keeping your nails trimmed and clean, keeping your hair clean and tied back, removing jewellery, wearing clean clothes and not going into work when you are feeling ill. Following these principles can prevent the spread of infections and ensure a more pleasant environment for everyone.

Knowledge Activity AC6.1

Find out about and read through your work setting's policy and procedure for personal hygiene. Describe in your own words the key principles of good personal hygiene.

....

....

....

....

....

....

....

....

....

....

....

AC6.2 Demonstrate good hand washing technique

Hand washing is one of the most important methods of preventing and controlling the spread of infections. A good hand washing technique includes the following:

H Hand rubbing, palm to palm
A Adequate time
N Nails washed
D Drying hands carefully

W Warm water used
A Avoiding touching surfaces after washing your hands
S Soap used
H Hands rinsed
I Items such as jewellery removed
N Not missing cleaning any areas of the hands
G Good, thorough drying of hands

Workplace Reflection

Reflect on the health or social care setting where you work and think about:

- the hand washing technique you use
- the hand washing techniques others use
- the correct hand washing technique to use
- why this is important
- the consequences of not doing so.

Assessment Activity AC6.2

For the assessment activity your assessor will observe you in your work setting. You will need to show your assessor that you are able to use a good hand washing technique. To do this you will need to be observed working; you must agree this with your manager.

AC6.3 Describe the correct sequence for hand washing

Effective hand washing involves following a sequence of steps; completing these every time you wash your hands will ensure that you minimise the spread of infection to others.

The World Health Organization has produced a series of diagrams outlining the correct sequence for effective and thorough hand washing. These involve the following ten steps:

1 Wet hands with warm water.
2 Apply soap.
3 Rub hands together, palm to palm.
4 Rub the right palm and then the left palm over the other hand with interlaced fingers.
5 Rub hands together, palm to palm with fingers interlaced.
6 Rub backs of hands together with fingers interlocked.
7 Rotationally rub left thumb clasped in right palm and then right thumb in left palm.
8 Rotational rub, backwards and forwards, with clasped fingers of right hand in left palm and then left hand in right palm.
9 Rinse hands with water.
10 Dry hands with paper towels.

Knowledge Activity AC6.3

Research effective hand washing and provide details about the correct sequence to follow. You may find the World Health Organization's website a useful source of information: http://who.int

AC6.4 Explain when and why hand washing should be carried out

It is important that health and social care workers are aware of when and why they should wash their hands. The table below provides examples of **when** hand washing should be carried out:

Before	After
You start work	You leave work
You come into contact with an individual	You have contact with an individual
Preparing and handling food	Preparing and handling food
Eating and drinking	Eating and drinking
Wearing gloves	Disposing of gloves

Health and social care workers must also be aware of the reasons **why** they must wash their hands. These are:

- to prevent the spread of infections
- to maintain good personal hygiene standards
- to comply with legislation
- to comply with the work setting's policies and procedures.

Knowledge Activity AC6.4

Explain, with examples, **when** and **why** hand washing should be carried out.

- When:

....

....

....

....

....

....

- Why:

....

....

....

....

....

AC6.5 Describe the types of products that should be used for hand washing

A number of products are available that should be used for hand washing. The diagram below identifies examples of some of these:

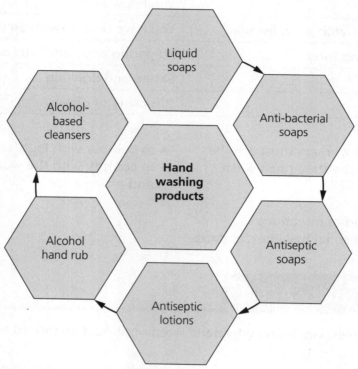

Figure 5 Products available for hand washing

Knowledge Activity AC6.5

Describe three different types of products that should be used for hand washing.

1) ....

....

....

....

2) ....

....

....

....

3) ....
....
....
....

AC6.6 Describe the correct procedures that relate to skincare

Maintaining good personal hygiene also involves health and social care workers looking after their skin. Frequent hand washing and the wearing of disposable gloves can make skin on the hands dry; not looking after your skin can result in it becoming sore and flaking, which increases both your vulnerability to infections and the risk of spreading infections to others. It is also important that any areas of your skin that are sore or have cuts are covered over.

Knowledge Activity AC6.6

Describe the correct skin care procedures to follow and that relate to:

● your hands:

....
....
....
....
....

● your skin:

....
....
....
....
....
....

Checklist of Skills Shown

✔ AC5.1 - Demonstrated correct use of PPE
✔ AC6.2 - Demonstrated good hand washing technique

Checklist of Knowledge Shown

✔ **AC1.1 - Explained** employees' roles and responsibilities in relation to the prevention and control of infection

✔ **AC1.2 - Explained** employers' responsibilities in relation to the prevention and control of infection

✔ **AC2.1 - Outlined** current legislation and regulatory body standards that are relevant to the prevention and control of infection

✔ **AC2.2 - Described** local and organisational policies relevant to the prevention and control of infection

✔ **AC3.1 - Described** procedures and systems relevant to the prevention and control of infection

✔ **AC3.2 - Explained** the potential impact of an outbreak of infection on the individual and the organisation

✔ **AC4.1 - Defined** the term 'risk'

✔ **AC4.2 - Outlined** potential risks of infection within the workplace

✔ **AC4.3 - Described** the process of carrying out a risk assessment

✔ **AC4.4 - Explained** the importance of carrying out a risk assessment

✔ **AC5.2 - Described** different types of PPE

✔ **AC5.3 - Explained** the reasons for use of PPE

✔ **AC5.4 - Stated** current relevant regulations and legislation relating to PPE

✔ **AC5.5 - Described** employees' responsibilities regarding the use of PPE

✔ **AC5.6 - Described** employers' responsibilities regarding the use of PPE

✔ **AC5.7 - Described** the correct practice in the application and removal of PPE

✔ **AC5.8 - Described** the correct procedure for disposal of used PPE

✔ **AC6.1 - Described** the key principles of good personal hygiene

✔ **AC6.3 - Described** the correct sequence for hand washing

✔ **AC6.4 - Explained** when and why hand washing should be carried out

✔ **AC6.5 - Described** the types of products that should be used for hand washing

✔ **AC6.6 - Described** correct procedures that relate to skincare

ISBN: 9781471806872
Impression number 1
Year 2015
© Maria Ferreiro Peteiro, 2015
First published 2015 by Hodder Education, an Hachette UK company, 338 Euston Road, London, NW1 3BH
All rights reserved. No part of this publication may be reproduced or transmitted in any form.
Typeset in: India
Printed in: Dubai

www.hoddereducation.co.uk

9781471806872